Spike Bennett

Quit Living In Your Mind

Proven Steps To Take To Stop Overthinking And Facing Reality

Table Of Contents

Introduction

The brain isn't a vessel to be filled, yet a fire to be encouraged.

The brain and its peculiarities of qualia and cognizance are non-material elements with data and data handling as their pith. They advanced into reality to assist with expanding the endurance opportunity of the species that have them.

Supporting mental cleanliness is just about as significant as cleaning up. Carving out an opportunity to comprehend the reason why you are feeling a specific way can ease.

The greatest wall you need to climb is the one you work for,never let your psyche work you out of your fantasies, stunt you into surrendering. Never let your psyche become the best impediment to progress. To get your psyche doing great, the rest will follow.

Bliss relies upon your mentality and disposition.The advanced psyche is overwhelmed and the cutting edge body is under-animated and overloaded.

Chapter 1

Positive Mindset

The circumstance we keep ourselves in. has driven us into a void of vulnerability, dread and agony. It very well may be difficult to explore through the new reality, yet there is an approach.

Keeping a positive mentality cleans each person off of uncertainties.You don't need to continue to stress over tomorrow or now,just keep your brain centered and manage any difficulties confronting you in the present.

Confidence is the way we esteem and see ourselves. It depends on our viewpoints and convictions about ourselves, which can at times feel truly hard to change.

Your confidence can influence whether you like and worth yourself as an individual can decide and state yourself.Recognise your assets and positives.Feel ready to attempt new or troublesome things.Show thoughtfulness towards yourself,move past mishaps without accusing yourself unreasonably.

Take the time you really want for yourself accept you matter and are great enough.Believe you merit happiness.Whatever has impacted your confidence, it's memorable and vital that you reserve the option to feel better about what your identity is. It could feel as though changing things will be troublesome, however there are heaps of things you can attempt to work on little by little.

Chapter 2

Healthy Living

As living animals, we want legitimate and normal nourishment, enough rest and hydration, moderate active work and social collaboration. In spite of the fact that getting along with others isn't a choice right now, it is feasible to remain associated with individuals by means of online entertainment, telephone and video calls, craftsmanship and leisure activities. These are the structure blocks of our profound soundness and usefulness. Ensure your rudiments are covered.

Practicing good eating habits doesn't generally mean severe weight control plans and removing everything under the sun. It is more about having adjusted dinners and consuming fats and sugar with some restraint.

This implies attempting to keep away from moment noodles all week long and guaranteeing you have a lot of products of the soil in your eating routine consistently.

Smart dieting makes your whole self feel better. It shows that you are requiring investment to mind by being aware of what you're placing into your body.

Keep yourself hydrated,make sure you're drinking around 2.5-3.5 liters of water a day. Giving your body sufficient water is critical as it assists with controlling internal heat level, keeps your joints greased up, conveys an adequate number of supplements to your cells, assists with forestalling contamination and keeps your organs working appropriately. Keeping yourself very much hydrated likewise helps you rest better and work on your temperament.

Peruse a book or a magazine. We as a whole need to escape from the squeezing worries of reality on occasion. On your next midday break move away from your PC and get a book in your #1 type or a side interest magazine. Perusing is a loosening up action that assists us with getting away from the tensions of our lives.

Get enough sleep.When you're caught up with working, proficient life is chaotic. We don't give our bodies as the need might arise to work completely. Pretty soon we think of ourselves as running on void. Rest isn't just great for the body, however it is likewise really great for the psyche. A very much refreshed body and mind can get extraordinary things done.

Getting sufficient rest is fundamental to remaining solid. Great quality rest sets you feeling better and gives your body time to rest and recuperate from the day. Furthermore, there are unending medical advantages that come from great rest: diminishing pressure, further developing mind capability (focus and memory), bringing down pulse and working on your resistant framework.

Chapter 3

Contemplation And Meditation

Contemplation and care rehearses are a sort of mental preparation that helps you to dial back your dashing considerations. It offers you the space to relinquish cynicism and quiet both your brain and body. There are numerous ways of rehearsing care or reflection, yet it for the most part includes a breathing practice with consciousness of the body and psyche.

This kind of training has demonstrated to be really useful while managing emotional wellness issues, stress and stress or even quieting yourself down by the day's end for better rest. One way or the other, evaluating this training is most certainly worth the effort.

It can seem like these propensities are excessively and excessively overpowering yet putting even one in one of them can assist with further developing your general prosperity. Begin little and in practically no time these means will be consistently integrated into your day to day daily schedule and you will be on the way towards a superior you.

Care is a natural human capacity to observe the present. At the point when one is careful, one is noticing and tolerating as opposed to staying away from and judging. In the condition of care we are allowed the chance to pick our responses and train versatility.

Strolling, perusing, eating, breathing - any action you truly do naturally consistently can be transformed into a care practice. Whenever you are having an espresso, focus on the shape and the temperature of the cup you are holding, smell the fragrance, relish each taste of your beverage. It's a simple method for partaking in the easily overlooked details and remaining careful.

Supporting mental cleanliness is pretty much as significant as cleaning up. Finding an opportunity to comprehend the reason why you are feeling a specific way can ease.

Meditation.The objective of reflection isn't to control your contemplations, it is to quit allowing your considerations to control you.

 Fast morning contemplation. A fast five or ten-minute contemplation every morning will assist with adjusting your brain for the bustling day ahead.Require several seconds to loosen up before you begin anticipating the evening. Ponder everything you are thankful for and give yourself some sure consolation.

Chapter 4

Keeping Good Company

Hanging out with friends and family can assist with keeping your brain at ease.Sharing stories that light giggling and optimism. Taking part in these valuable minutes with loved ones isn't just charming, it's likewise gainful to your wellbeing.

Individuals who invest energy with loved ones track down better ways of adapting to stress.Many individuals utilize their loved ones as a pressure cushion, discussing their concerns as opposed to looking for negative survival strategies like drinking liquor, smoking or doing drugs.Older grown-ups with bigger informal communities have a decent verbose memory, better mental capabilities and a lower allostatic load, which is the mileage on the body and mind from being worried. Having a decent connection with conjugal accomplices, grown-up youngsters, kin, and companions add to these positive wellbeing impacts.

The everyday encouragement given by friendly ties improves your mental prosperity. One investigation discovered that individuals who view their loved ones as steady detailed a more noteworthy feeling of significance throughout everyday life and felt like they had a more grounded feeling of direction.

Having old buddies and a solid social encouraging group of people can ease stress.People who examined troublesome times in their lives had a lower heartbeat and pulse when they had a companion close by. It is never simple to Relinquish a relationship. We gain such a great amount from companions and friends and family, that we frequently clutch connections that are as of now not really great for us habitually or steadfastness.

Conversing with somebody you trust can bring about various good results, for example, getting another point of view on things and getting consolation and support.Feeling heard and comprehended can be extremely soothing for some people.This can be a prepared specialist, a relative, a companion or a school instructor.

Call a close buddy. Reconnect with somebody you had the opportunity to converse with in some time. Occupied lives impede fellowship. Profession, family, obligation causes us to fail to remember the people who are unforgettable to us. Companions become ancient remnants of the past. In the online entertainment age, individuals will generally monitor companions through different virtual entertainment locales, however seldom at any point get the telephone.

Chapter 5

New Habits

Practice your body for a blissful brain. A tiny amount of exercise will make a huge difference to lessening pressure. Indeed, even an energetic stroll in the first part of the day will empower and rouse you for the day ahead.Set your mindfulness for fairly sooner than anticipated and hit the black-top.Save time by setting up the prior night. Spread out your activity garments so you can kick off negligible planning time.

Set aside some margin to plunk down and dairy out your concerns, tensions or even only considerations for the afternoon; just let your contemplations stream out normally until you have nothing else you need to compose. In this cutting edge period, things move so rapidly, our considerations notwithstanding. Recording things assists you with easing back your

viewpoints and recognizing them a piece
better.

Composing is a restorative movement. In only
a couple of moments, you can compose your
contemplations, stresses, appreciation, or
whatever else rings a bell. Keep the diary close
to your bed and make a propensity for
composing a couple of passages or even
sentences every prior night you nod off.

Journaling is an extraordinary method for
sitting with your viewpoints and truly knowing
about the thing you're thinking and the way that
you're feeling. It's a second you can take to
interface with yourself once more and is a very
liberating practice.

Dealing with yourself frequently begins with
finding the right living climate, one that you feel
like you can flourish in.Learn how to get your
psyche by plunking down and working out each
of the considerations in your mind. It is a
compelling strategy for essentially delivering
your considerations with the goal that you can
intellectually inhale and handle things better.

Get a piece of paper and work out the
contemplations that are all squeezing for your

consideration. The thought isn't to examine the considerations or fix them, yet to give those contemplations an exit so you can continue on with your day without focusing on them forcefully. This can seem to be a clothing rundown of considerations, or a journal section.

A short time later, go ahead and close your diary or tear up the paper as a feature of your pressure on the executives. You don't have to clutch your message, yet it assists with seeing the statement of what you're clutching intellectually. Moreover, this training is exceptionally intense to do around evening time before sleep time. So many of us battle to rest sufficiently with numerous contemplations returning and forward, and this activity before bed can permit us to enter a more profound degree of rest.

Hiking is demonstrated to have numerous medical advantages, going from actual activity you get when out on the path, too close to home or mental alleviation that comes from being in nature.
Being in nature can support your temperament and work on emotional well-being. Investing quality energy in nature diminishes pressure, quiets uneasiness, and can prompt a lower

chance of discouragement. As well as having emotional well-being benefits, being outside opens up your faculties to your environmental factors and works on your tactile discernment. Taking in the sights, scents, and sensations of nature has so many medical advantages it might be recommended by a specialist.
You don't need to act like a lone ranger next time you trim up your hiking boots. Get a companion, neighbor, or relative for more fun on the path.Hiking with an accomplice, or even in a gathering, can work on the strength and soundness of your connections. Since hiking goes from a very provoking move to an easygoing approach to investing energy outside, it's an extraordinary method for reinforcing the fellowships or bonds you have with your partners. Whether it's with a more youthful kin, neighborhood companion, or even a grandparent, hiking a path together can bring you closer and assist with building solid connections.

The warm daylight all over, the breeze racing through the trees above, and the delicate hearty feel of the path under your boots. Not exclusively are these encounters charming to have, yet they're great for you, as well.

Hiking is frequently exceptionally viable for facilitating nervousness and discouragement, and a treatment choice is open to by far most individuals. As a matter of fact, there are various reasons hiking is a particularly incredible method for feeling much improved, which we'll frame beneath.

Hiking assists you with disengaging from everyday life activities.Chances are, you are continually blasted by improvements from the second you awaken until the second your head raises a ruckus around town. Your telephone, television and radio continually buzz with messages, data and amusement, and you most likely don't have a lot of chances to consider your contemplations unobtrusively. Yet, to move away from this, you should simply all lash on your hiking boots and hit the path. Rather than our areas, homes and workplaces, wild regions are for the most part tranquil and serene. This assists you with shedding a portion of the pressure brought about by day to day existence.

Detaching from your everyday life in this manner can be extremely supportive and assist with decreasing your nervousness and sorrow. Clearly, you ought to in any case carry your

telephone alongside you for the good of
security, yet perhaps you ought to switch off
the ringer for some time - essentially until you
return to your vehicle.

Chapter 6

Create Time For Yourself

Plan time for yourself. At the point when we finish up our schedules for the afternoon, we ordinarily don't plan for time for ourselves. We recall significant telephone calls, gatherings, and cutoff times. Next time you begin finishing up your everyday schedule, plan blocks of time for yourself. Plan an opportunity toward the beginning of the day for some activity. Plan an opportunity at night to visit with companions.

Turn off from innovation. Individuals will generally get their telephone first thing while awakening. Then, at that point, work starts. Browsing email prompts answering to email and in a flash, now is the ideal time to prepare up and get for work. Let the hardware be until you've given yourself an opportunity to plan for

the afternoon. Set aside a few minutes for
breakfast which is the main dinner of the day
and save the email for the finish of your wake-
up routine.

One more component of the world we live in
today is the steady correspondence we have
with one another through online entertainment.
And keeping in mind that this is perfect in
numerous ways, it can get overpowering and
diverting. PC screens and computerized
gadgets emanate a great deal of blue light
which can add to dry eyes and computerized
eye strain.

In this way, it's critical to require a couple of
moments or hours daily where you switch off
all just a tad. You can utilize this opportunity to
peruse a book or do some planting or perhaps
dance around a little. Simply invest energy with
yourself, away from the remainder of the
computerized world.

Take a pre-made feast to have for lunch. We
don't invest sufficient energy dealing with our
bodies. Lunch consists of eating out, which
isn't solid all the time. Pre-put together your
lunch the prior night and sustain your body with

nutritious food. Remove your lunch from your work area and unwind.

Make your end of the week about you, not work. Many individuals bring their work back home with them and never truly get a free day. Take time toward the end of the week to do things you appreciate. Invest more energy with your family, not with your work space. Take a scaled down excursion. Limit interruptions by fighting the temptation to browse email. Partake in side interests or exercises that you appreciate. Join a neighborhood sports group or volunteer at your #1 association.

Advise yourself that you are spectacular. Try not to let cutoff times and a requesting position get you down. Help yourself to remember everything you have achieved and don't become involved with issues or disappointments. You are not your work and finding an opportunity to recall things that characterize you as a person outside your work will contribute altogether to an inward feeling of harmony.

Your body and psyche are your most significant resources. To traverse every day both should be kept with everything looking great. Make sure to surrender yourself to a tune consistently by doing a portion of the exercises referenced previously. Plan time for you as well as your brain and body will be much obliged.

Dealing with your wellbeing and prosperity is fundamental to guaranteeing your whole self is calm. This assists you with having a superior point of view and assists you with getting past everyday undertakings. Periodically, we get so up to speed in every one of the stressors and errands that surface, we neglect to require one moment to focus on our wellbeing and prosperity.

Conclusion

To quit living in your mind,every individual requires a positive mentality and great self esteem.You ought to move toward disagreeableness in a more sure and useful manner. You think the best will occur, not absolutely terrible.

Positive reasoning frequently begins with self-talk. Self-talk is the wearisome stream of certain considerations that go through your psyche. These modified contemplations can be positive or negative. A part of your self-talk comes from reasoning and reason. Other self-talk might emerge from misinterpretations that you make in light of absence of data or assumptions because of assumptions of what might occur.

Assuming the contemplations that go through your mind are generally bad, your point of view is more probable skeptical. In the event that your contemplations are for the most part certain, you're reasonably a positive thinker.

Positive reasoning furnishes individuals with expanded life span,lower paces of depression,lower levels of misery and pain,better mental and actual prosperity and better adapting abilities during difficulties and seasons of pressure.

Hopeful individuals will generally live better lifestyles,they get more actual work, follow a better eating regimen, and don't smoke or savor liquor excess.If you need to turn out to be more hopeful and take part in more certain reasoning, first distinguish aspects of your life that you as a rule ponder, whether it's work, your day to day drive, life changes or a relationship. You can begin little by zeroing in on one region to move toward in a more sure manner. Consider a positive idea to deal with your pressure rather than a negative one.

Permit yourself to smile or chuckle, especially during inconvenient times.Look for humor in ordinary happenings. At the point when you can snicker at life, you feel less worried.

Plan to rehearse for about 30 minutes on most days of the week. You can similarly separate it into 5-or 10-minute bits of time during the day.Exercise can emphatically influence mind-set and lessen pressure. Follow a strong eating routine to fuel your mind and body.Get sufficient rest. Also, learn procedures to oversee pressure.

Encircle yourself with positive individuals.Guarantee those in your life are positive, consistent people you can depend upon to offer steady direction and analysis.Pessimistic individuals might build your feeling of anxiety and make you question your capacity to oversee pressure in sound ways.

Practice positive self-talk. Begin by following one basic rule:Don't express anything to yourself that you wouldn't agree with any other individual. Be delicate and empowering with yourself. On the off chance that a negative idea occurs to you, assess it normally and answer with insistences of why you are great. Ponder things you're appreciative for in your life.

Clearness assists you with pushing through uncertainty.
At the point when you're unfocused and occupied, beginning questioning yourself is simple. Mental lucidity assists you with seeing

yourself genuinely and non-critically. Rather than stressing over others' thought process of you, be reasonable and focused.

www.ingramcontent.com/pod-product-compliance
Lightning Source LLC
Chambersburg PA
CBHW070728160726
48003CB00006BA/2411